M000297196

THE SPIRIT WHO EMPOWERS

A Gospel Centered Exploration of
ACTS

MIKE COSPER

LifeWay Press®
Nashville, Tennessee

Item: 005798731
ISBN: 978-1-4627-7661-0
Dewey decimal classification: 231.3
Subject headings: HOLY SPIRIT \ BIBLE. N.T. ACTS--STUDY AND TEACHING \ DISCIPLESHIP

Eric Geiger
Vice President, LifeWay Resources

Ed Stetzer & Trevin Wax
General Editor

Brian Dembowczyk
Managing Editor

Michael Kelley
Director, Groups Ministry

Sam House
Content Editor

We believe that the Bible has God for its author; salvation for its end; and truth, without any mixture of error, for its matter and that all Scripture is totally true and trustworthy. To review LifeWay's doctrinal guideline, please visit lifeway.com/doctrinalguideline.

Unless otherwise noted, all Scripture quotations are taken from the Christian Standard Bible®. Copyright 2017 by Holman Bible Publishers. Used by permission.

For ordering or inquiries, visit lifeway.com; write LifeWay Small Groups; One LifeWay Plaza; Nashville, TN 37234-0152; or call toll free (800) 458-2772.

Printed in the United States of America.

Groups Ministry Publishing
LifeWay Resources
One LifeWay Plaza
Nashville, Tennessee 37234-0152

TABLE OF CONTENTS

ABOUT THE GOSPEL PROJECT

Some people see the Bible as a collection of stories with morals for life application. But it's so much more. Sure, the Bible has some stories in it, but it's also full of poetry, history, codes of law and civilization, songs, prophecy, letters—even a love letter. When you tie it all together, something remarkable happens. A story is revealed. One story. The story of redemption through Jesus. This is *The Gospel Project.*

When we begin to see the Bible as the story of redemption through Jesus Christ, God's plan to rescue the world from sin and death, our perspective changes. We no longer look primarily for what the Bible says about us but instead see what it tells us about God and what He has done. After all, it's the gospel that saves us, and when we encounter Jesus in the pages of Scripture, the gospel works on us, transforming us into His image. We become God's gospel project.

ABOUT THE WRITERS

MIKE COSPER
Mike Cosper is the founder and director of Harbor Media, where he develops podcasts that help Christians navigate a post-Christian world. Previously he served for 16 years as one of the founding pastors of Sojourn Community Church in Louisville, Kentucky, where he oversaw Sojourn Music—a collective of musicians writing songs for the local church. He is the author of four books, including (most recently) *Recapturing the Wonder.*

HOW TO USE THIS STUDY

Welcome to *The Gospel Project*, a gospel-centered small-group study that dives deep into the things of God, lifts up Jesus, focuses on the grand story of Scripture, and drives participants to be on mission. This small-group Bible study provides opportunities to study the Bible and to encounter the living Christ. *The Gospel Project* provides you with tools and resources to purposefully study God's Word and to grow in the faith and knowledge of God's Son. And what's more, you can do so in the company of others, encouraging and building up one another. Here are some things to remember that will help you maximize the usefulness of this resource:

GATHER A GROUP. We grow in the faith best in community with other believers, as we love, encourage, correct, and challenge one another. The life of a disciple of Christ was never meant to be lived alone, in isolation.

PRAY. Pray regularly for your group members.

PREPARE. This resource includes the Bible study content, three devotionals, and discussion questions for each session. Work through the session and devotionals in preparation for each group session. Take notes and record your own questions. Also consider the follow-up questions so you are ready to participate in and add to the discussion, bringing up your own notes and questions where appropriate.

RESOURCE YOURSELF. Make good use of the additional resources available on the Web at gospelproject.com/additionalresources and search for this specific title. Download a podcast. Read a blog post. Be intentional about learning from others in the faith. For tips on how to better lead groups or additional ideas for leading this Bible study, visit: ministrygrid.com/web/thegospelproject.

GROUP TIME. Gather together with your group to discuss the session and devotional content. Work through the follow-up questions and your own questions. Discuss the material and the implications for the lives of believers and the mission to which we have been called.

OVERFLOW. Remember…*The Gospel Project* is not just a Bible study. *We* are the project. The gospel is working on us. Don't let your preparation time be simply about the content. Let the truths of God's Word soak in as you study. Let God work on your heart first, and then pray that He will change the hearts of the other people in your group.

SESSION 1

THE SPIRIT COMES

"If the love of God poured forth in our hearts by the Holy Spirit, who is given to us, is able to make of many souls but one soul and of many hearts but one heart, how much more are the Father and the Son and Holy Spirit but one God, one Light, one Principle?"[1]

AUGUSTINE

INDIVIDUAL STUDY

On a gorgeous spring day about a decade ago, I found a gift on my front porch. I had been out walking my old dog when I found it—a simple brown paper gift bag containing a loaf of really great bread, butter, jam, some pricey cheeses, and a book, also wrapped in brown paper. It was genuinely one of the most thoughtful gifts I've ever received, and it clearly came from someone who knew me well. This person knew I liked weird modern fiction, crusty bread, and good butter. He or she knew where I lived and that it was my birthday.

Gifts are powerful things. The trouble with my gift, though, was that it was anonymous. Whoever gave it to me did not leave a card, a signature, nor any clear signs as to who it came from. My wife and I puzzled over it that evening as we tore the bread into pieces and smeared it with butter and strawberry preserves. "Who sent it?" we asked a thousand times. Neither of us had a clue, nor do we know to this day.

What gift story do you have to tell—about a gift received or a gift given?

What are the pros and cons of an anonymous gift? Of a gift from a known giver?

Unlike my anonymous gift, we don't have to ask who sent the gift of the gospel. The gospel not only comes from God, it's spread by God's own handiwork. While the Book of Acts communicates the spread of the gospel from "Jerusalem, in all Judea and Samaria, and to the end of the earth" (Acts 1:8) through the apostles and the churches they planted, the primary Actor in the Book of Acts—spreading the gospel, building up the church, and healing the sick—is God Himself, specifically in the person of the Holy Spirit, giving gifts of life and redemption and advancing God's kingdom.

Not only does God reconcile us to Himself in Christ's death and promise us eternal life in His resurrection, He gives us the greatest gift we can imagine in the Holy Spirit—the gift of Himself. The Holy Spirit comes to indwell every believer in Christ, to empower the spread of the gospel throughout the world, and to build the community of faith. He has come to point sinners to Christ and to strengthen Christ-followers for Christlike living in the world and to the ends of the earth.

The Spirit Indwells Believers

During Jesus' final days on earth, both before His crucifixion and up to His ascension, He began promising the disciples that another Counselor would come to carry on His work. He said, "If you love me, you will keep my commands. And I will ask the Father, and he will give you another Counselor to be with you forever. He is the Spirit of truth. The world is unable to receive him because it doesn't see him or know him. But you do know him, because he remains with you and will be in you" (John 14:15-17).

This is a wonderfully trinitarian statement—the Son asks the Father to send the Counselor. But before we get the wrong idea and somehow think that these three Persons are somehow independent of one another, Jesus adds, "I will not leave you as orphans; I am coming to you" (John 14:18). Just as the Son and the Father are one, the Son and the Spirit are one. So though Jesus goes away to the Father, the Counselor comes and Jesus is still present.

Such is the mystery of the Trinity as revealed in Scripture. God the Father, God the Son, and God the Holy Spirit are distinct yet one at the same time, and we always need to hold these two revealed truths together—God is one; God is Trinity. We can't make sense of this. It's not a riddle to solve but a wonder to behold in faith.

So when Jesus promised the Holy Spirit, He was also promising Himself. This makes sense of the fact that Scripture tells us Jesus is seated at the right hand of the Father (see Eph. 1:20; Heb. 8:1; 12:2) and He is with us always, "to the end of the age" (Matt. 28:20). When the Holy Spirit is sent to us, God is present, and that, of course, means that Jesus Himself is present with us.

How should the revelation of God as Trinity shape the way we pray?

It makes it all encompassing. I've been thinking wrongly in that God is for the huge (first-glance) seemingly hopeless things (without Him), then Jesus for the "everyday" things & forgiveness of sin & the

The way we worship? *Holy Spirit for wisdom, discernment, understanding, self control etc.*

Yes, worship to all three. Mindblowing for sure. At least we know what we don't understand. I'm thankful to know the Holy Spirit should be acknowledged.

Here's how the Book of Acts describes the coming of the Holy Spirit:

> [1] When the day of Pentecost had arrived, they were all together in
> one place. [2] Suddenly a sound like that of a violent rushing wind came
> from heaven, and it filled the whole house where they were staying.
> [3] They saw tongues like flames of fire that separated and rested on
> each one of them. [4] Then they were all filled with the Holy Spirit and
> began to speak in different tongues, as the Spirit enabled them.
> ACTS 2:1-4

How bewildering it all must have been for the disciples as they obeyed Jesus' final words. For the next ten days, the disciples gathered together in an upstairs room in Jerusalem and prayed and waited for the Father's promise to be fulfilled. (See Acts 1:4-5,12-14.) And then, without warning, the Spirit rushed into the world, rushed into the room, and rushed into their hearts as He manifested Himself in what appeared like flickering flames of fire resting on each one of those present in the room.

In the coming of the Spirit, Jesus' promise to be with us always makes sense, as does the prophet Joel's promise that one day God would pour out His Spirit on "all humanity" (Joel 2:28). Likewise, the coming of the Spirit reveals the unique role that Christ's followers will play in the world—not merely as a faithful group that exists to remember what Jesus did but as God's agents for good in the world and as the very vessels God will use to carry out His mission. God's kingdom will continue to advance as God continues His work through His church in His world through His Holy Spirit.

What thoughts or expectations do you have regarding the filling of the Holy Spirit in a believer's life? *That we will be changed from the inside out.*

How should the indwelling of the Spirit change the way believers live? *Our thinking and behavior should change. We begin to see people and situations through different lenses — through God's perspective.*

2 The Spread of the Gospel

The apostle Peter, filled with the Spirit, stood before a massive crowd and preached this sermon:

22 "Fellow Israelites, listen to these words: This Jesus of Nazareth was a man attested to you by God with miracles, wonders, and signs that God did among you through him, just as you yourselves know. 23 Though he was delivered up according to God's determined plan and foreknowledge, you used lawless people to nail him to a cross and kill him. 24 God raised him up, ending the pains of death, because it was not possible for him to be held by death. 25 For David says of him:

I saw the Lord ever before me;
because he is at my right hand,
I will not be shaken.
26 Therefore my heart is glad
and my tongue rejoices.
Moreover, my flesh will rest in hope,
27 because you will not abandon me in Hades
or allow your holy one to see decay.
28 You have revealed the paths of life to me;
you will fill me with gladness
in your presence.

29 "Brothers and sisters, I can confidently speak to you about the patriarch David: He is both dead and buried, and his tomb is with us to this day. 30 Since he was a prophet, he knew that God had sworn an oath to him to seat one of his descendants on his throne. 31 Seeing what was to come, he spoke concerning the resurrection of the Messiah: He was not abandoned in Hades, and his flesh did not experience decay. 32 "God has raised this Jesus; we are all witnesses of this. 33 Therefore, since he has been exalted to the right hand of God and has received from the Father the promised Holy Spirit, he has poured out what you both see and hear. 34 For it was not David who ascended into the heavens, but he himself says:

The Lord declared to my Lord,
'Sit at my right hand
35 until I make your enemies your footstool.'
36 "Therefore let all the house of Israel know with certainty that God has made this Jesus, whom you crucified, both Lord and Messiah."

³⁷ When they heard this, they were pierced to the heart and said to
Peter and the rest of the apostles: "Brothers, what should we do?"
³⁸ Peter replied, "Repent and be baptized, each of you, in the name of Jesus
Christ for the forgiveness of your sins, and you will receive the gift of the Holy
Spirit. ³⁹ For the promise is for you and for your children, and for all who are far
off, as many as the Lord our God will call." ⁴⁰ With many other words he testified
and strongly urged them, saying, "Be saved from this corrupt generation!"
ACTS 2:22-40

What implications should this sermon have on how we share the gospel?

That we shouldn't judge how "bad/evil" someone is, we all need forgiveness of our sins. Also, the Holy Spirit gave Peter the boldness & the words — He'll do the same for us

Peter couldn't contain himself. He nearly exploded with this sermon, urgently pointing to Jesus as the Messiah. But this wasn't simply Peter talking here, it was Peter filled with the Spirit.

What we learn by looking at the Book of Acts is that the Spirit compels us to speak out. The mission of the church is a reflection of the heart of the Holy Spirit, who is more eager than anyone to celebrate the work of the Father and the Son.

Knowing this should dramatically shift the way we think about sharing the gospel. If you're like me, you might find yourself struggling at times to speak up, to know when to share your faith, or to initiate conversations about Jesus. Often techniques are suggested for making those conversations easier. But perhaps the easiest way to be more bold in sharing the gospel is by seeking to be filled with the Spirit. (See Eph. 5:18-19; cf. Acts 13:50-52.)

What are some struggles that keep Christians from sharing the gospel with others? *Afraid of being shut down, perhaps people lashing out about a loss or hardship and ask where God was, ask questions we can't answer.*

How does the filling of the Holy Spirit overcome these struggles and empower our evangelism? *He gives us the boldness and the words for that particular person & their situation.*

3 The Spirit Builds Community

When the Spirit comes, He brings life and growth, and this growth resembles that of a tree with its branches and roots. On one hand, the kingdom spreads into the world in visible, extensive ways characteristic of the church's mission. The momentum of this growth is overflowing and outward. But the kingdom also grows in often unseen ways with an inward momentum resulting in depth, stability, and holy relationships. This inward growth was also visible in Acts 2.

> [41] So those who accepted his message were baptized, and that day about three thousand people were added to them. [42] They devoted themselves to the apostles' teaching, to the fellowship, to the breaking of bread, and to prayer. [43] Everyone was filled with awe, and many wonders and signs were being performed through the apostles. [44] Now all the believers were together and held all things in common. [45] They sold their possessions and property and distributed the proceeds to all, as any had need. [46] Every day they devoted themselves to meeting together in the temple, and broke bread from house to house. They ate their food with joyful and sincere hearts, [47] praising God and enjoying the favor of all the people. Every day the Lord added to their number those who were being saved.
>
> ACTS 2:41-47

In this passage, there are many signs of God's grace and God's work. There are signs and wonders, referring to miracles such as healing the sick and casting out demons that characterized both Jesus' ministry and the ministry of the apostles, but there are more subtle miracles as well. These believers shared their possessions, they sold what they had in excess in order to give away the proceeds to those in need among them, and they met regularly and shared meals.

This kind of abundant, intense, and dedicated community life should be seen for the miracle it is. This sort of thing doesn't just happen. Most of the time, when you force people to live in tight, communal circumstances, the opposite occurs. Proximity leads to conflicts, and conflicts lead to strengthened borders. "Good fences make good neighbors," as they say, and that's because there's less potential for conflict when what's mine is mine and what's yours is yours.

In Acts 2, however, this newly formed community presses into one another's lives, and the boundaries around possessions and wealth disappear. Moved by the Spirit, each believer's interests shifted from self to the good of the community of faith, and they began sharing all they had. They were sharing meals, sharing space, and sharing life.

When the Holy Spirit takes up residence in our hearts, we begin to overflow with love for God and love for our neighbors, especially those who share our faith. These twin loves for God and others fuel the whole of the Christian life. It is love of God that leads us to bear witness to the gospel around the world, and it is love of our brothers and sisters that leads us to develop rich, deeply committed relationships with God's people.

Too often we emphasize one love over the other. When we focus only on the community of faith, we can lose touch with the wonder of God—sharing the gospel keeps that wonder fresh and alive in our hearts. Likewise, when we focus only on bearing witness to Jesus without developing any real relationships with other Christians, we find ourselves without accountability and often lacking the humility and gentleness that come as a result of being deeply known and deeply loved by the people around us.

What's displayed in Acts 2 comes as a result of the gift of God's Spirit. It cannot be controlled or manipulated or manufactured. It only comes when open hearts, stirred to faith by the gospel, receive this gift from the Father and the Son and are filled by Him. And so we seek this Spirit-transformed life not merely by imitating these behaviors but by seeking God's presence, by asking Him to fill us with His Spirit and renew our love for Him, His Word, and His gospel.

How have you experienced the deep community of faith in the name of Jesus and through the indwelling of the Holy Spirit?

Through Bible study, prayer and small groups

What are some ways we can contribute to this Spirit-filled community of faith?

GROUP STUDY

Warm Up

If you've not heard this Bible story before, you will be mesmerized by its details. If you have heard this story all your life, then try to re-imagine it, blow the dust off, and hear it afresh. Remember what had happened in the previous few weeks to the disciples. Not long before, Jesus had arrived in Jerusalem like a King arriving for His coronation. The whole city greeted Him, hailing the new King of the Jews. A few days later, however, He died, hung on a cross with a sign bearing the same title. But three days after that, He rose from the dead.

The disciples seemed bewildered by all that had taken place. Rome remained in control of Jerusalem. There would be no new Israel, no freedom from the tyranny of their oppressors. And yet, so much more had happened. Jesus had risen from the dead. They'd shared meals and conversations with Him. They'd touched His scars. They'd seen Him appear behind locked doors in a glorified body that was at once recognizable and unrecognizable, familiar and new. And they'd seen Him taken up into the heavens with the promise that He would come again in the same way. But first, the Spirit would come as He had promised.

How would you explain the purpose of the Holy Spirit in your life?

To guide, teach me, to give me wisdom, understanding, discernment, to convict me of sin, to empower me with strength and boldness to do God's will.

In what ways can you be sure you're being led by the Holy Spirit?

By knowing God and His Word.

"If the love of God pervades our hearts, without a doubt it
will soon engender affection for our neighbor as well." [2]

BEDE

Discussion

1. How should the revelation of God as Trinity shape the way we pray? The way we worship? *All three should be acknowledged in both prayer and praise. We should also have a worship of gratitude for each*

2. What thoughts or expectations do you have regarding the filling of the Holy Spirit in a believer's life? *That He would guide me - convict me of wrong choices, give me a way of escape, give me wisdom & discernment as well as boldness and strength to do what He leads me to do.*

3. How should the indwelling of the Spirit change the way believers live? *We should live much more obedient and selfless lives, not wanting to either stifle or grieve the Holy Spirit.*

4. What implications should this sermon have on how we share the gospel? *That at any given time, we can be assured - when called, the Holy Spirit will totally equip & empower us. The harvesting & growing is God's.*

5. What are some struggles that keep Christians from sharing the gospel with others? *Fear - of rejection, of being embarrassed, of ridicule, backlash and questions of "where was this 'good God' when ..."*

6. How does the filling of the Holy Spirit overcome these struggles and empower our evangelism? *By giving us boldness to still share in spite of our fears and giving us the words to say, giving us the strength not to take the backlashing and rejection personally*

7. How have you experienced the deep community of faith in the name of Jesus and through the indwelling of the Holy Spirit? *Through bible study groups, prayer groups and small groups.*

8. What are some ways we can contribute to this Spirit-filled community of faith? *By assisting by working/helping (i.e. yard work, cleaning, repair, etc). Being Jesus' hands & feet.*

Conclusion

While receiving the gift of the Holy Spirit is a once-and-for-all occasion when we put our faith in Jesus, being filled with the Spirit is the lifelong responsibility of the believer, turning to God in faith and joy and learning to live with a deeper and more abiding trust in Him. As we are filled, then, we should overflow—to our friends, our neighbors, our families, and more—with the love and joy that come from abiding in the gospel of our Savior. This is our greatest way of bearing witness: not the begrudging "I-should-do-this-though-I-feel-awkward" kind of evangelism but the natural reaction of a joy-filled heart to redemption. This comes only as a gift, only as we're filled with the Spirit, and only as we turn our own attention to this good news.

Spend some time praying this for you and for your group:

"God, thank You for Your Holy Spirit who empowers us to be Your witnesses on earth. Help us during times when we are called to do things we aren't able to do on our own to remember it is You who provides us with all that we need through Your Spirit. May we always trust in the Spirit who changes us to be more like You."

1. Augustine, *Tractates on the Gospel of John*, 39.5, quoted in *Acts*, ed. Francis Martin, with Evan Smith, vol. 5 in *Ancient Christian Commentary on Scripture: New Testament* (IVP, 2014) [WORDsearch].
2. Bede, *Commentary on the Acts of the Apostles*, 2.44, quoted in *Acts*, ed. Francis Martin, with Evan Smith, vol. 5 in *Ancient Christian Commentary on Scripture: New Testament* [WORDsearch].
3. Henry Blackaby and Melvin Blackaby, *Experiencing the Spirit: The Power of Pentecost Every Day* (Colorado Springs: Multnomah, 2009) [eBook].

"Will God ever ask you to do something you're not able to do? The answer is yes—all the time! It *must* be that way for God's glory and kingdom. If we function according to our ability alone, we get the glory; if we function according to the power of the Spirit within us, God gets the glory. He wants to reveal *Himself* to a watching world."[3]

HENRY BLACKABY AND MELVIN BLACKABY

NOTES

SESSION 2

A SPIRIT-EMPOWERED MINISTRY

"Once the heart of creation beats with the heart of the Creator
of all the nations, it will be impossible to remain silent." [1]

RODNEY M. WOO

INDIVIDUAL STUDY

There are circumstances in our lives that lead us to make risky decisions, to do brave things, because of a sudden burst of boldness and audacity—like the mother who sees her child in harm's way and confronts a grizzly bear. Firefighters, policemen, and EMS workers often make bold and fearless decisions in moments of crisis.

But the stakes aren't always life and death. It takes boldness to pursue a career of almost any kind, and it takes boldness to try to be an artist or an entrepreneur in light of the fact that so many others fail in these pursuits. Romance and love also require a certain boldness. In a world where marriage seems so fragile and the odds of sticking together seem so slim, it takes boldness to choose to say "I do." But in each of these cases, boldness leads to something good. Boldness saves lives. It allows us to follow our dreams and pursue our sense of calling. It leads to love and reconciliation and to the deep community that can only thrive in a family.

What bold acts have you taken in your life, and what were the results?

What circumstances led to such boldness?

The Christian life demands a certain boldness as well. We live in a world where faith and spirituality are constantly resisted, where the vast majority of the ideas that shape our world treat God as though He were superfluous or nonexistent. To be a Christian in the world we live in today demands a certain kind of boldness in the face of this spiritual resistance. Christians believe some audacious things: God made the world; sin broke it; and God is reconciling it all to Himself through Jesus, His Son, who lived, died, and rose on the third day. Simply confessing this belief makes a stark and bold claim upon the world, and living out this belief demands even more boldness.

But Christian boldness isn't something we simply have to "muster up" for ourselves; rather, it comes through faith in Jesus and through the gift of His Holy Spirit, who empowers and emboldens us to live for the glory of our Savior. If we are convinced that the gospel is true, then we must act on what we believe, praying to God for boldness and then proclaiming what we know to be true. We should find ourselves compelled to say and do bold things for the sake of the gospel.

1 Do Good and Give Glory

In Acts 3–4, we see a story of Spirit-empowered boldness when Peter and John healed a crippled man and had to deal with some of the consequences of following in Jesus' steps.

3:1 Now Peter and John were going up to the temple for the time of prayer at three in the afternoon. 2 A man who was lame from birth was being carried there. He was placed each day at the temple gate called Beautiful, so that he could beg from those entering the temple. 3 When he saw Peter and John about to enter the temple, he asked for money. 4 Peter, along with John, looked straight at him and said, "Look at us." 5 So he turned to them, expecting to get something from them. 6 But Peter said, "I don't have silver or gold, but what I do have, I give you: In the name of Jesus Christ of Nazareth, get up and walk!" 7 Then, taking him by the right hand he raised him up, and at once his feet and ankles became strong. 8 So he jumped up and started to walk, and he entered the temple with them—walking, leaping, and praising God. 9 All the people saw him walking and praising God, 10 and they recognized that he was the one who used to sit and beg at the Beautiful Gate of the temple. So they were filled with awe and astonishment at what had happened to him.

....

4:5 The next day, their rulers, elders, and scribes assembled in Jerusalem 6 with Annas the high priest, Caiaphas, John, Alexander, and all the members of the high-priestly family. 7 After they had Peter and John stand before them, they began to question them: "By what power or in what name have you done this?"
8 Then Peter was filled with the Holy Spirit and said to
them, "Rulers of the people and elders:
9 If we are being examined today about a good deed done to a disabled man, by what means he was healed, 10 let it be known to all of you and to all the people of Israel, that by the name of Jesus Christ of Nazareth, whom you crucified and whom God raised from the dead—
by him this man is standing here before you healthy. 11 This Jesus is
the stone rejected by you builders,
which has become the cornerstone.
12 There is salvation in no one else, for there is no other name
under heaven given to people by which we must be saved."
ACTS 3:1-10; 4:5-12

In this story are two separate instances of Spirit-empowered ministry: the act of healing the lame man and the act of bearing witness to the Jewish leadership. In each case, Peter and John needed the Spirit to enable their work. Trusting the Spirit's presence and power, Peter offered the lame man healing—a profoundly better gift than silver and gold. He offered this gift not for its own sake but "in the name of Jesus Christ of Nazareth." Healing and health came to this man so that others would hear about Jesus.

> **How can our good deeds done in Jesus' name lead to others hearing about Jesus?**

In a public space, for all to see, Peter told the crippled man to get up and walk, and the man took Peter's hand, stood, and began walking, leaping, and praising God. Then, seizing this amazing opportunity to speak to the gathering crowd that was amazed at the miracle, Peter preached yet another sermon about Jesus being the crucified and risen Messiah, in whose name this healing had occurred. (See Acts 3:11-26.)

After being arrested for this spectacle (see 4:1-3), Peter and John were called before the Jewish leaders to explain themselves. Peter could easily have sought to save his own life, to deny any knowledge of the events, or to minimize the involvement of Jesus' name. (Let's not forget that denying Jesus was something Peter had struggled with before.) But in this moment, he confronted them directly. He defied their hatred of Jesus and was clear in accusing them of the murder of the Messiah. Peter was not trying to be a hero here with his bold stand and defiance of the religious authorities. He was simply telling them the truth about who Jesus is—the cornerstone of all creation, the only Source of salvation in the world.

> **What risks are involved in proclaiming Jesus as the only way of salvation in the world?**

> **What attitudes and motivations should we resist as we share the gospel of Jesus with others?**

② Devotion to Jesus

The Jewish leaders knew they were facing a crisis. They had executed Jesus as a heretic, and yet, His followers continued to carry out miraculous work in His name. Acts 4:13-18 tells us how they sought to manage the crisis.

> ¹³ When they observed the boldness of Peter and John and realized that they were uneducated and untrained men, they were amazed and recognized that they had been with Jesus. ¹⁴ And since they saw the man who had been healed standing with them, they had nothing to say in opposition. ¹⁵ After they ordered them to leave the Sanhedrin, they conferred among themselves, ¹⁶ saying, "What should we do with these men? For an obvious sign has been done through them, clear to everyone living in Jerusalem, and we cannot deny it. ¹⁷ But so that this does not spread any further among the people, let's threaten them against speaking to anyone in this name again." ¹⁸ So they called for them and ordered them not to speak or teach at all in the name of Jesus.
>
> ACTS 4:13-18

Rather than own their obvious failure to recognize Jesus and rather than acknowledge the miraculous work being done in their midst, they chose to try and silence it, not unlike how they paid the soldiers to say Jesus' body was stolen from the tomb by His disciples. (See Matt. 28:11-15.) This reaction wasn't an anomaly either.

Throughout the past two thousand years, efforts have been made by religious, political, and cultural leaders to ban the name of Jesus and to silence His followers. At times, that effort is driven by violence. At other times, though, the effort to silence the name of Jesus comes under a more subtle guise. It comes from certain corners of academia, where the historicity of Jesus is discredited. It comes from political leaders and activists who pressure Christians to abandon orthodoxy and accommodate the fashionable ethics of our time. It comes from friends and neighbors who wish we'd talk about anything else but Jesus.

What are some ways you have experienced the pressure to minimize your witness to Jesus?

To resist the pressure to minimize Jesus, we need three things. First, we need to keep our eyes on Jesus—on who He is and what His life, death, and resurrection have accomplished for us. This sounds simple, maybe even simplistic, but it's not. The Bible is replete with admonitions to "remember" our God. We are terribly forgetful creatures, and we are immersed in a world that's telling counter-stories for every aspect of our faith. We need to remember constantly the name of Jesus if we want to be prepared to declare the name of Jesus under duress.

Second, we need the gathering of God's people. When we gather with the church, we're reminded of our hope, of our confession of faith, and of the Savior who draws the people of God together. (See Heb. 10:23-25.) We're also reminded that we're citizens of a different kind of kingdom and under a different kind of authority than the political and social kingdoms we live amongst.

Third, we need the boldness that comes from the filling of the Holy Spirit. According to Acts 4:19-22, Peter and John were prepared for this moment, and filled with the Spirit of God, they answered their oppressors with faith and boldness, refusing to deny Jesus in order to satisfy the Jewish leaders.

> [19] Peter and John answered them, "Whether it's right in the sight of God for us to listen to you rather than to God, you decide; [20] for we are unable to stop speaking about what we have seen and heard."
>
> [21] After threatening them further, they released them. They found no way to punish them because the people were all giving glory to God over what had been done. [22] For this sign of healing had been performed on a man over forty years old.
>
> ACTS 4:19-22

Empowered by God's Spirit (see Acts 4:8), Peter and John refused to obey the command of the Jewish leaders, appealing to their role as witnesses of what they had seen and heard. Likewise, one of our most powerful tools for sharing the gospel is our own story of how the gospel changed us.

How can your story of hearing and believing the gospel open doors for sharing the gospel with others?

3 Boldly Pray and Preach

After standing up to the Sanhedrin, the apostles went back to the church. Acts 4:23-31 records what happened next.

> [23] After they were released, they went to their own people and reported everything the chief priests and the elders had said to them. [24] When they heard this, they raised their voices together to God and said, "Master, you are the one who made the heaven, the earth, and the sea, and everything in them. [25] You said through the Holy Spirit, by the mouth of our father David your servant:
> Why do the Gentiles rage
> and the peoples plot futile things?
> [26] The kings of the earth take their stand
> and the rulers assemble together
> against the Lord and against his Messiah.
> [27] "For, in fact, in this city both Herod and Pontius Pilate, with the Gentiles and the people of Israel, assembled together against your holy servant Jesus, whom you anointed, [28] to do whatever your hand and your will had predestined to take place. [29] And now, Lord, consider their threats, and grant that your servants may speak your word with all boldness, [30] while you stretch out your hand for healing, and signs and wonders are performed through the name of your holy servant Jesus." [31] When they had prayed, the place where they were assembled was shaken, and they were all filled with the Holy Spirit and began to speak the word of God boldly.
> ACTS 4:23-31

There's an important connection here between bold prayer and bold ministry. After a string of Spirit-filled ministry victories, even in the context of an unjust imprisonment, the church responded by seeking the face of God in worshipful prayer. These Christians were keenly aware that all that had happened—the healing, the bold confrontation with the Jewish leaders, the favor of the crowds—was the work of God, and more specifically, the work of the Holy Spirit. So in response, the church turned back to God and asked Him to continue His work. They prayed for continued boldness, for healing, signs, and wonders, and they prayed for these things to happen in the name of Jesus.

Do you think most ministry-oriented prayers are reactive or proactive? Why do you think that is the case?

Why should we pray both in response to circumstances and in preparation for our acts of ministry?

This is the model for Spirit-filled ministry: There was an awareness of who God is—the One who made the heaven, the earth, and sea—and an awareness of what God had done—He had spoken through David and anointed Jesus—and this served as the background for what they asked. Their prayer could be paraphrased like this: "Lord, we know who You are, we know what You've spoken, and we know who You've sent. Because of this, we believe You can deal with the threats in front of us, and we ask that You keep blessing our ministry in the name of Jesus." This prayer models knowledge of God and dependence upon God.

We can follow in their footsteps by dedicating as much time and energy to the prayers that surround our ministry as we do to the work itself. By taking prayer as seriously as we take the "actual" work—be it music ministry, feeding people in need, preaching, or sharing the gospel with friends and neighbors—we put the work of ministry in its proper place. Bold ministry requires bold prayer, and bold prayer enables bold ministry. It is God's work that makes the deaf hear, the blind see, and the dead walk again, and yet these miracles happen only when people of faith step out in Jesus' name and touch, speak, and love their neighbors. It is para-doxical, but it isn't contradictory. It's the mystery of life in the Spirit. God works as we work. We work as He works. In prayer, these efforts are united.

What things might keep us from praying for God's power and boldness in the ministry of our group/church?

How does praying through the story of God's work in Scripture, in history, and in our lives embolden our prayers?

GROUP STUDY

Warm Up

Whether you are a vocational pastor or a volunteer, it is easy to get focused on the latest task or the latest crisis. It's easy to lose sight of the big picture and forget God in the midst of ministry.

We are so tied up in the mechanics and busyness of ministry that we lose sight of the spiritual reality that stands behind it—that all of our efforts are empty if the Spirit doesn't empower, sustain, and continue them through His work. Nothing leads to burnout and weariness faster than ministry in our own strength.

The Christians in Acts 4 saw that God's work began long before them, and they were merely participating in that bigger story. This perspective humbled them—knowing that God's story was much larger than their own—and empowered them. They saw how God had faithfully carried out the work for centuries. And so, the people were able to go out with boldness. The pressure was off of them; God had been doing and would continue this work.

In what ways does the story of God's work in Scripture, in history, and in your life embolden your prayers and keep you focused on God?

"Those men who received power from God never used that power as if it were their own but referred the power to him from whom they received it; for the power itself could never have any force except through the name of him who gave it. And so both the apostles and all the servants of God never did anything in their own name but in the name and invocation of Christ." [2]

JOHN CASSIAN

Discussion

1. How can our good deeds done in Jesus' name lead to others hearing about Jesus?

2. What risks are involved in proclaiming Jesus as the only way of salvation in the world?

3. What attitudes and motivations should we resist as we share the gospel of Jesus with others?

4. What are some ways you have experienced the pressure to minimize your witness to Jesus?

5. How can your story of hearing and believing the gospel open doors for sharing the gospel with others?

6. Do you think most ministry-oriented prayers are reactive or proactive? Why do you think that is the case?

7. Why should we pray both in response to circumstances and in preparation for our acts of ministry?

8. What things might keep us from praying for God's power and boldness in the ministry of our group/church?

Conclusion

Like the first Christians, we face spiritual resistance. Most of us haven't had to risk our lives (though some Christians in the world certainly do), but we do risk ridicule, mockery, and dismissal from an unbelieving culture and from unbelieving friends, neighbors, and family. When confronted by a world that makes us feel strange or ridiculous for our faith, may we be filled with the Spirit and His words, may we remain devoted to our Savior, and may we pray for the boldness to proclaim His gospel and His praises.

One of our most powerful tools for sharing the gospel is our story with the gospel. What we've seen and heard, the ways we've experienced the power and presence of God, the change we've witnessed in ourselves and in our church family—these things can't really be argued or debated. Spirit-empowered evangelistic boldness will often flow from our stories, and these will often be the most compelling way we can share the good news about Jesus with others.

Spend some time praying this for you and for your group:

> "God, thank You for giving us a story to share and for empowering us to share it. May we never lose sight of what You have done in our lives, what we have seen You do in the lives of others, and the awesome opportunity and responsibility we have been given to share this news with others. Help us to be both bold and gracious in our approach."

1. Rodney M. Woo, *The Color of Church* (Nashville: B&H, 2009), 3.
2. John Cassian, *On the Incarnation of the Lord Against Nestorius*, 7.19, quoted in *Acts*, ed. Francis Martin, with Evan Smith, vol. 5 in *Ancient Christian Commentary on Scripture: New Testament* (IVP, 2014) [WORDsearch].
3. Kay Arthur, *God, How Can I Live?* (Eugene, OR: Harvest House, 2004), 92.

"If you do not plan to live the Christian life totally committed to knowing your God and to walking in obedience to Him, then don't begin, for this is what Christianity is all about. It is a change of citizenship, a change of governments, a change of allegiance. If you have no intention of letting Christ rule your life, then forget Christianity; it is not for you."[3]

KAY ARTHUR

NOTES

SESSION 3

THE SPIRIT OF TRUTH AND GENEROSITY

"Believers are never told to *become* one; we're *already* one, and we're expected to act like it." [1]

JONI EARECKSON TADA

INDIVIDUAL STUDY

In early 2016, Hamdi Ulukaya, founder of the Chobani Yogurt company, made front page news with a business decision. To celebrate the company's success, Ulukaya called together his company's employees and announced that he was giving 10 percent of the company's stock to be distributed amongst them. The result was some of these employees—working a blue-collar manufacturing job at a dairy company—would be millionaires.

Contrast this with the story of Martin Shkreli, the CEO of a pharmaceutical company, who raised the price of a medication from $13.50/pill to $750/pill. Shkreli was universally loathed for this decision. And yet, it was perfectly legal and permissible.

What separates Shkreli and Ulukaya isn't just their character on display in their business decisions; it's their sense of the kind of world we live in. What should we expect from the world? And how should we act as we go about our business in it?

> **How might you expect these two business leaders to view the world differently and live differently from each other?**

For Ulukaya, the world would seem to be an abundant place, and the proper response to success, wealth, and thriving would be extending it to others, especially to those who made the success possible. For Shkreli, the world would seem to have a scarcity of resources, so the more one can acquire the better, no matter the cost. In other words, it might destroy your reputation, but if it makes you rich, then it is worth it.

The Bible is clear that the world is a place of abundance, and it calls us to a life of joyful generosity in response, whether that is with our money, our possessions, our time, or our very lives.

Generosity should be a defining characteristic of the church because God is generous. The Father gave His Son. The Son gave His life. The Father and the Son gave the Spirit. And the Spirit gives the followers of Christ hearts of generosity. The Spirit works through these hearts to bring unity to the body of Christ through their loving support for one another.

1 Inspire Generosity

The Holy Spirit inspired radical generosity in the early church, which inspired them to share all they had and to care for one another's needs:

> [32] Now the entire group of those who believed were of one heart and mind, and no one claimed that any of his possessions was his own, but instead they held everything in common. [33] With great power the apostles were giving testimony to the resurrection of the Lord Jesus, and great grace was on all of them. [34] For there was not a needy person among them because all those who owned lands or houses sold them, brought the proceeds of what was sold, [35] and laid them at the apostles' feet. This was then distributed to each person as any had need.
> ACTS 4:32-35

To understand what's happening here, we need to see it in the light of Jesus' statements about relationships between believers. In Mark 3:31-35, Jesus redefines the way believers should prioritize their relationships: "His mother and his brothers came, and standing outside, they sent word to him and called him. A crowd was sitting around him and told him, 'Look, your mother, your brothers, and your sisters are outside asking for you.' He replied to them, 'Who are my mother and my brothers?' Looking at those sitting in a circle around him, he said, 'Here are my mother and my brothers! Whoever does the will of God is my brother and sister and mother.'"

We live in an age when people are more tribal and individualistic, and the idea of denying one's own family isn't nearly as foreign, shocking, or offensive as it was in the first century. But in Jesus' day, these comments were truly scandalous. He was disrupting the primary way people thought about loyalty, family, and community. To be sure, His comments weren't an outright rejection of His family but rather a redefinition of family. "Whoever does the will of God is my brother and sister and mother," He said. Our primary bond should not be blood but faith in God.

How have you experienced the blessing of the family of God?

In Acts 4, this same dynamic is at work. These new Christians now found themselves part of this new family, and the bond that they once ascribed to blood relatives and siblings was applied to their brothers and sisters in Christ. If someone had a need, they responded with radical generosity. Those who were wealthy and had more than they needed sold their resources and properties in order to provide for others in their new family.

It's important not to misunderstand what was happening here. This isn't a call to poverty, and it isn't a demand for Christians to sell everything they have and give it to the poor. In fact, it isn't a demand at all; it's an invitation.

Generosity is a fruit of God's grace, something that an individual should feel compelled to do from their own internal motivations. (See 2 Cor. 9:7.) While in one way this understanding liberates us from any legalism around giving, it simultaneously heightens our expectations for giving. Because generosity flows from the heart, it is a tangible way of seeing the condition of the heart. This is why Jesus said, "For where your treasure is, there your heart will be also" (Matt. 6:21).

Love for the family of God is the centerpiece of the passage. We might be shocked and scandalized by the radical steps these believers took, but we should be more stunned by the love that motivated them. When we examine our own lives, we should ask how we've made space for that kind of generosity with other Christians. In the body of Christ, we are all now brothers and sisters, and when a family member has a need, it should inspire the family to respond with love, care, and radical generosity.

Why might biblical stories and examples of radical generosity make us nervous?

What would a life of radical generosity in the church look like today?

2 See Generosity and Greed

The heart is always what concerns God when it comes to our giving, not the gift itself. Joyful giving, whether it's a lot or a little, whether it's all we have or just a portion, is something that God delights in. By contrast, reluctant giving, constrained giving, or giving that's meant as a display of our own righteousness—a way to impress the people around us—reveals the heart as well. It reveals a heart that is unmoved by grace, or a self-interested heart.

> [4:36] Joseph, a Levite from Cyprus by birth, the one the apostles called Barnabas (which is translated Son of Encouragement), [37] sold a field he owned, brought the money, and laid it at the apostles' feet.
>
> ....
>
> [5:1] But a man named Ananias, with his wife Sapphira, sold a piece of property. [2] However, he kept back part of the proceeds with his wife's knowledge, and brought a portion of it and laid it at the apostles' feet.
>
> ACTS 4:36–5:2

There's a familiar story here, and one that many of us can probably identify with on some level. Joseph, more popularly known as Barnabas, moved by the gospel and by his love for the church, chose to sell a field he owned and give the money to the apostles for them to distribute to those in need.

We can imagine that there was some kind of applause or at least acknowledgment for what was genuinely and certainly a generous action. This recognition, whether it came from the apostles or the disciples as a whole, was what subsequently motivated Ananias. It was not that he wanted to be generous but that he wanted to be seen as generous.

When Ananias and his wife, Sapphira, laid their gift at the apostles' feet, the problem wasn't that they held back a proportion of the profit but that they presented it as if this were the whole value of the parcel they sold. (We'll see this clearly in verses 3-9 later.) So the issue was not the amount they gave or the amount they withheld; it was their dishonesty. The lie revealed the truth of Ananias and Sapphira's hearts—they weren't giving out of generous hearts but greedy ones, and their greed wasn't simply material, it was also spiritual. They wanted to give so that they would be seen as radically generous. They wanted the praise of the crowd.

What are some ways dishonesty might creep into our giving?

How can we guard ourselves against dishonesty in giving?

Jesus was often critical of this kind of religious performance. While teaching on giving, He said:

> [1] "Be careful not to practice your righteousness in front of others to be seen by them. Otherwise, you have no reward with your Father in heaven. [2] So whenever you give to the poor, don't sound a trumpet before you, as the hypocrites do in the synagogues and on the streets, to be applauded by people. Truly I tell you, they have their reward. [3] But when you give to the poor, don't let your left hand know what your right hand is doing, [4] so that your giving may be in secret. And your Father who sees in secret will reward you."
>
> MATTHEW 6:1-4

Ananias and Sapphira's lies were birthed from a selfish desire either to compete (perhaps with Barnabas) or a selfish desire to impress the apostles and disciples. Their giving was decidedly not born from generous hearts eager to love God and serve His church. As a result, their gift didn't bring life; it destroyed it.

For us, their story invites us to examine our own motivations in how and why we give. Are we giving with joyful hearts? Are we giving in response to God's goodness to us? Or are we giving to ensure our names show up on the right lists? Are we generous because we're joyful or because we want to display generosity?

How can reflecting on the gospel of Jesus lead us to joy in generous giving for the benefit of others in need?

3 Judgment and Discipline

What happens next to Ananias, and later Sapphira, is rather shocking:

> [3] "Ananias," Peter asked, "why has Satan filled your heart to lie to the Holy Spirit and keep back part of the proceeds of the land? [4] Wasn't it yours while you possessed it? And after it was sold, wasn't it at your disposal? Why is it that you planned this thing in your heart? You have not lied to people but to God." [5] When he heard these words, Ananias dropped dead, and a great fear came on all who heard. [6] The young men got up, wrapped his body, carried him out, and buried him. [7] About three hours later, his wife came in, not knowing what had happened. [8] "Tell me," Peter asked her, "did you sell the land for this price?"
>
> "Yes," she said, "for that price."
>
> [9] Then Peter said to her, "Why did you agree to test the Spirit of the Lord? Look, the feet of those who have buried your husband are at the door, and they will carry you out." [10] Instantly she dropped dead at his feet. When the young men came in, they found her dead, carried her out, and buried her beside her husband. [11] Then great fear came on the whole church and on all who heard these things.
>
> ACTS 5:3-11

Ananias was confronted for his deception, and he dropped dead. His wife did too. Some might think this was a harsh punishment, but it was a sign of the depth and severity of their sin, and ours too, for that matter. This wasn't about an accounting error, and really, it wasn't about money at all. It was about the unity of the family of God and how sin violates the trust, intimacy, and communion of His family.

Because of the gospel, these Christians were living sacrificial and generous lives and enjoying the fruit of that generosity. For those with more than they needed, they took joy in giving to others. For those in need, they took joy in having their needs met.

Ananias and Sapphira wanted the credit for a greater sacrifice than they were willing to make. It seems unlikely that they'd have dropped dead if they'd either truly given it all or been honest about keeping a portion for themselves. But judgment came because they pursued their own glory rather than God's, their own good rather than the church's.

How might this biblical narrative feed into some misconceptions people have about the God of the Bible?

What truths of the Bible would help us respond to those misconceptions?

The Spirit's judgment and the discipline that accompanied it were necessary in the life of the church. Ananias and Sapphira's story is a dramatic example, but discipline comes in many forms, and often in subtle ones. It comes not because God is a cranky and intolerant overseer, but because He loves His church and longs for its purity. (See Heb. 12:5-11.)

The discipline we experience may not be as severe as Ananias and Sapphira's (we should certainly hope not), but sin always has consequences, and the pain of those consequences is one way God purifies and shapes us.

This happens on both large and small scales. Big, earth-shattering relational sins like adultery have obvious consequences, but less obvious and more subtle sins—white lies, greed, lust—take their toll as well. Their consequences—lost trust, lost health, lost desire—are all invitations to repent and be transformed and changed by the Spirit of God.

Throughout the New Testament, we see examples of Christians being called to confront one another in their sin and, if one is unrepentant, to disassociate from them. (See Matt. 18:15-17; 1 Cor. 5.) When this is a Spirit-guided process, it is one of both great seriousness and great joy, especially as it leads to sinners walking in repentance. The church deepens its purity as it listens to the Spirit, grows in conviction over its sins, and is healed of them by His power.

What do the deaths of Ananias and Sapphira say about the purity of the church?

What role do the people of God have in preserving the purity of the church?

GROUP STUDY

Warm Up

> "We must be absolutely clear as to what Ananias' sin was. It was not casual deception. Rather, he feigned a deeper spiritual commitment than he had. We share Ananias' sin not when others think we are more spiritual than we are, but when we try to make others think we are more spiritual than we are. Examples of Ananias' sin today include: creating the impression we are people of prayer when we are not; making it look like we have it all together when we do not; promoting the idea that we are generous when we are so tight we squeak when we smile; misrepresenting our spiritual effectiveness." [2]
> —R. KENT HUGHES

The difference between Barnabas and Ananias was their sense of what kind of world we live in. Barnabas had a sense that the world is abundant; he could share what he had with confidence because he knew that all he had came from God and that he could rely on God and God's people for his needs. Ananias lived in a world of scarcity; he didn't just cling to his wealth, he grasped for adulation and applause. Grasping at money and fame, Ananias soon found that he would have neither.

What modern day implications can we take from this story?

> "A lack of generosity refuses to acknowledge that your assets are not really yours, but God's." [3]
>
> TIMOTHY KELLER

Discussion

1. How have you experienced the blessing of the family of God?

2. What would a life of radical generosity in the church look like today?

3. What are some ways dishonesty might creep into our giving?

4. How can we guard ourselves against dishonesty in giving?

5. How can reflecting on the gospel of Jesus lead us to joy in generous giving for the benefit of others in need?

6. How might this biblical narrative feed into some misconceptions people have about the God of the Bible?

7. What truths of the Bible would help us respond to those misconceptions?

8. What role do the people of God have in preserving the purity of the church?

Conclusion

We live in an abundant world, as seen in the lavish way God made the world and in the way He pursues and provides for His people—whether a ram in a bush, a lamb at Passover, or manna in the desert, and of course, in the life, death, and resurrection of Jesus. In this abundant world, giving somehow yields more than keeping. As our supreme example, in giving away His life, Jesus became exalted above every name. (See Phil. 2:5-11.)

In following Jesus, we're invited to do the same: not clinging to what we have but giving it away, becoming a servant, and allowing God to multiply it for His good and glory in His church and in the world around us. The Holy Spirit's presence in our lives should inspire such radical generosity, transforming our hearts to mirror Jesus' own so that we don't cling to what's "ours" by rights but give it away to those in need.

Spend some time praying this for you and for your group:

> "God, thank You for giving Your Son for us. He in turn gave up heavenly riches to share His inheritance with all those who trust in Him. Help us to give with pure and generous hearts, sharing our resources with those in need. Use the things we give to expand Your kingdom."

1. Joni Eareckson Tada, *Glorious Intruder: God's Presence in Life's Chaos* (Colorado Springs: Multnomah, 1989), 82.
2. R. Kent Hughes, *Acts: The Church Afire*, in *Preaching the Word* (Wheaton: Crossway, 2008) [WORDsearch].
3. Timothy Keller, *Generous Justice: How God's Grace Makes Us Just* (New York: Dutton, 2010), 91.
4. David J. Williams, *Acts*, in *Understanding the Bible Commentary Series* (Grand Rapids: Baker, 2016) [WORDsearch].

"One of the most remarkable features of life among the early believers was their unity. This is expressed here in the words they were 'one in heart and mind,' a typically Hebraic turn of phrase indicating their complete accord ... This unity, ...was demonstrated, as it had been from the first, in their readiness to meet one another's needs, their love of neighbor." [4]

DAVID J. WILLIAMS

NOTES

SESSION 4

A SPIRIT-EMPOWERED TESTIMONY

"God ... gives us assurance and confirms all his promises as definitely as, for example, a man holding an object in his hands is certain that he has it. In the same way faith grasps the promise of God, which is invisible, and clings to it as though it were visible." [1]

PETER RIEDEMANN

INDIVIDUAL STUDY

Years ago, a friend of mine was invited to take part in a panel discussion at a songwriter's conference for Christian artists. During the question-and-answer portion of the panel, someone asked what they look for in a song: "How do you know a song is good?" Answers varied, but my friend's answer had a sort of puritan starkness to it: "I'm looking for songs that prepare people for their encounter with death."

To him, what mattered most about a song wasn't so much the musical or even poetic content, though of course those elements have their place. Instead, his greatest concern was that the song clearly held out the gospel as the ultimate hope in both life and death for the Christian. A catchy tune doesn't comfort someone at a hospital bedside or a garden graveside. If lyrics don't address the ultimate issues of life, death, and resurrection, then they don't offer sustaining power for those who are suffering.

How do you determine what counts as a "good song"?

How have certain songs comforted you during times of suffering?

The gospel declares that death is far from the end, and it re-frames our lives and work within the promise that God is restoring all things through Christ Jesus. Whether in joy or suffering, thriving or languishing, our lives' meaning and purpose is found in a larger and more glorious story being written by the Creator of the cosmos. And this knowledge empowers the Christian to encounter suffering, persecution, hardship, embarrassment, ridicule, and even death with an incredible boldness.

In this session, we will see how God's Holy Spirit empowers the followers of Christ to endure suffering for the sake of Christ. Whether that suffering takes the form of false accusations, death, or other variations, our faithful witness in the midst of suffering is a testimony to Jesus Christ, who came to fulfill the Law and the Prophets and to save us from our sin. When we suffer in faith, we are following in the footsteps of our Savior and bearing witness to His worth above all things, even our very lives.

1 False Accusations

One of the earliest and most powerful stories of Christians staring down suffering and death comes from Acts 6–7, where Stephen, a disciple of Jesus, is persecuted for his testimony about Jesus. The story begins this way in Acts 6:8-15.

> [8] Now Stephen, full of grace and power, was performing great wonders and signs among the people. [9] Opposition arose, however, from some members of the Freedmen's Synagogue, composed of both Cyrenians and Alexandrians, and some from Cilicia and Asia, and they began to argue with Stephen. [10] But they were unable to stand up against his wisdom and the Spirit by whom he was speaking. [11] Then they secretly persuaded some men to say, "We heard him speaking blasphemous words against Moses and God." [12] They stirred up the people, the elders, and the scribes; so they came, seized him, and took him to the Sanhedrin. [13] They also presented false witnesses who said, "This man never stops speaking against this holy place and the law. [14] For we heard him say that this Jesus of Nazareth will destroy this place and change the customs that Moses handed down to us." [15] And all who were sitting in the Sanhedrin looked intently at him and saw that his face was like the face of an angel.
>
> ACTS 6:8-15

Stephen, filled with the Holy Spirit, gets a reputation for performing signs and wonders while testifying to who Jesus is amongst the Jews. As a result, he attracts the attention of men who want to come and argue with him, challenging him and hoping to stop his testimony. But because of his wisdom and because he's filled with the Spirit of God, their efforts fall short.

This is a consistent theme in the Book of Acts: ordinary men like Stephen and Peter taking up debates with well-educated clergy and winning. Their unfair advantage in these debates is twofold. First, they're on the side of the truth (which makes winning any debate much easier). And second, they're filled with the Holy Spirit, which gives them supernatural wisdom in what to say and when.

As the story progresses, Stephen is taken before the Sanhedrin, a body of religious leaders who oversaw the Jewish community. There, his opponents resort to low and dirty tactics, lying about what Stephen has been preaching and teaching.

What comparisons do you see between Stephen and Jesus thus far?

We shouldn't be surprised if we experience something similar. Stephen was accused of speaking blasphemy against the temple and against the law found in the Old Testament. In our case, what's more likely is that we'll be accused of hateful speech, of bias and bigotry, simply because we hold to traditional beliefs about the value of human life, the meaning of marriage, and the origins of sexuality. Even if we never utter a judgmental word, we might find ourselves accused. Here in Acts 6, we see that this is the nature of opposition to Christianity. It thrives on exaggeration, distortion, and lies in an attempt to discredit the work of the gospel.

How have you seen false accusations being leveled against Christians?

How have you seen such opposition become a blessing?

What role does the Holy Spirit play in our response to opposition?

What is our responsibility to prepare for the reality of opposition?

2 Fulfillment of the Old Testament

Eventually Stephen is called on to speak, and when he does, he delivers a stark rebuke and a clear testimony to Jesus as the fulfillment of the Old Testament, which they have accused him of blaspheming.

> [44] "Our ancestors had the tabernacle of the testimony in the wilderness, just as he who spoke to Moses commanded him to make it according to the pattern he had seen. [45] Our ancestors in turn received it and with Joshua brought it in when they dispossessed the nations that God drove out before them, until the days of David. [46] He found favor in God's sight and asked that he might provide a dwelling place for the God of Jacob. [47] It was Solomon, rather, who built him a house, [48] but the Most High does not dwell in sanctuaries made with hands, as the prophet says:
>
> [49] Heaven is my throne,
> and the earth my footstool.
> What sort of house will you build for me?
> says the Lord,
> or what will be my resting place?
> [50] Did not my hand make all these things?
>
> [51] "You stiff-necked people with uncircumcised hearts and ears! You are always resisting the Holy Spirit. As your ancestors did, you do also. [52] Which of the prophets did your ancestors not persecute? They even killed those who foretold the coming of the Righteous One, whose betrayers and murderers you have now become. [53] You received the law under the direction of angels and yet have not kept it."
>
> ACTS 7:44-53

When Stephen spoke about where God dwells, he and his audience had the whole history of the tabernacle and temple in mind, both their construction and destruction. God had never been confined to these dwelling places, which no one in Israel disputed, but Stephen went further and told them that they were missing the point of what was happening in Israel at that time. God had indeed come back to Israel, but He wasn't manifesting Himself in the temple; He was there in flesh and blood. Jesus had come, and they had killed Him.

By saying this, not only did Stephen confront them as those who killed Jesus, he lumped them in with all of those who had been unfaithful to God in Israel's history. Just as the unfaithful members of Israel had killed the prophets, their first-century sons had killed the One to whom the prophets had pointed. They killed Jesus—God incarnate—and now they were persecuting His church, where God the Holy Spirit lives in the hearts and praises of the followers of Christ.

> How would you describe your experience of God dwelling within the church?

Often when we read the Scriptures, we like to imagine ourselves on the side of the "good guys." But in a story like this, it's wise to stop and ask ourselves how we might be like the angry members of the Sanhedrin. We all come to accept a certain set of attitudes about how God might be at work and what we expect Him to do. When something comes along that defies those expectations, we tend to get stiff-necked, sticking to our way of seeing and thinking rather than learning from what God is doing. And when we do that, we miss out.

The Book of Acts is, in many ways, a big party. God has come to dwell with Israel again, and He's confirming it through the many miracles and wonders happening all over the region. The Sanhedrin's stubborn refusal to see it because they weren't expecting it to look so lowly and a-political means they not only miss out on the party but they miss out on the presence of God.

> What is the relationship between the temple, the Holy Spirit, and the people of God?

> What are some ways we might get in the way of Christians obeying the leading of the Spirit?

3 A Christlike Death

In Acts 7:54-60, we see the response to Stephen was swift and terrible:

> 54 When they heard these things, they were enraged and gnashed their teeth at him. 55 Stephen, full of the Holy Spirit, gazed into heaven. He saw the glory of God, and Jesus standing at the right hand of God. 56 He said, "Look, I see the heavens opened and the Son of Man standing at the right hand of God!"
> 57 They yelled at the top of their voices, covered their ears, and together rushed against him.
> 58 They dragged him out of the city and began to stone him. And the witnesses laid their garments at the feet of a young man named Saul.
> 59 While they were stoning Stephen, he called out: "Lord Jesus, receive my spirit!" 60 He knelt down and cried out with a loud voice, "Lord, do not hold this sin against them!" And after saying this, he died.
>
> ACTS 7:54-60

There are three things worth pausing on in this final scene in Stephen's life, all of which illustrate the way his death was a testimony to Jesus.

First, notice that God was with Stephen in the midst of this trial.

As the pressure of persecution got more and more intense, so did God's sustaining provision—Stephen looked into heaven and saw God's glory with Jesus standing at God's right hand. Stephen couldn't deny Jesus' lordship in that moment because he saw it so clearly, perhaps more clearly than he ever had before. So he cried out in joy and in worship, even as the mob raged against him. God provides what we need as we need it, and when suffering and trials come into our lives, we can be confident that God will supply the strength, support, and encouragement we need in order to remain faithful through them.

How have you experienced the Holy Spirit sustaining your faith in the midst of trials?

Second, we see Stephen doesn't let the fact that he's right make him judgmental or arrogant.

As Stephen dies, he cries out, "Lord, do not hold this sin against them!" Like Jesus, he cried out for mercy for his persecutors. He wanted them to believe in Jesus, not simply to believe him. Preaching, evangelizing, and contending for the faith must come from a heart of love and compassion for the lost, not from an ego that simply wants to win.

Third, as the crowd gathered stones to kill him, they piled their cloaks at the feet of a Jew named Saul.

This Saul, we know from a few chapters later, would become one of the church's most violent persecutors. But then he became one of the church's leading church planters and theologians, whom we know as the apostle Paul. His presence at this moment reminds us that we never quite know what will result from our ministries and our words.

Spirit-filled Christians find themselves doing many strange and wonderful things. Perhaps nothing is so strange and powerful as the fearlessness with which they can face suffering and death. A supernatural strength sustains them, and it's just as powerful when they face a mob as when they face cancer or Ebola. Empowered by the Spirit and looking with hope to Jesus, we have a confidence that overshadows the power of death. (See 1 Cor. 15:51-58.) Stephen died at the hands of persecutors, but he died with great confidence because Jesus is alive, the grave is defeated, and in His world, we have nothing to fear.

How have you seen faithful suffering encourage believers? Open doors to sharing the gospel with unbelievers?

How is the good news of Jesus displayed in examples of radical forgiveness?

GROUP STUDY

Warm Up

Many would point to Stephen's death and call it a failure. No converts, no confessions that Jesus is Lord; only increased animosity toward the followers of Jesus. But of course, this was far from the end of Stephen's influence and story.

The fact that this story is included in the Book of Acts tells us that someone witnessed it, someone knew it mattered, someone was impacted by these words. Very likely, that someone was Paul himself, who partnered with Luke (the author of Acts) on many missionary ventures later in the book. It seems like Stephen's prayer for mercy for his persecutors found a most unlikely answer in the conversion of the ringleader for his execution.

How have you seen opposition become a blessing?

In what ways is Stephen's life an example of how believers should live?

"I am not tired of my work, neither am I tired of the world, yet, when Christ calls me home, I shall go with gladness." [2]

ADONIRAM JUDSON

Discussion

1. How have you seen false accusations being leveled against Christians?

2. What role does the Holy Spirit play in our response to opposition?

3. What is our responsibility to prepare for the reality of opposition?

4. How would you describe your experience of God dwelling within the church?

5. What is the relationship between the temple, the Holy Spirit, and the people of God?

6. What are some ways we might get in the way of Christians obeying the leading of the Spirit?

7. How have you experienced the Holy Spirit sustaining your faith in the midst of trials?

8. How have you seen faithful suffering encourage believers? Open doors to sharing the gospel with unbelievers?

Conclusion

The history of the church is rich with stories of Christians who, emboldened by the Spirit, faced suffering and death while testifying to Jesus. Missionaries have died while going to share the gospel with hostile people. Countless martyrs from around the world and throughout the ages have faced torture and death for their faith in the risen Savior.

In almost every case, these tragedies don't end in the silencing of the gospel or the stemming of its spread; in fact, it's quite the opposite. The persecution of the church and the martyring of its people is like the pruning of a plant. It grows stronger, richer, and more deeply-rooted as a result. And that pattern can be traced all the way back to the first Christians, beginning with Stephen.

Spend some time praying this for you and for your group:

> "God, help us remember that as we face ridicule and persecution for
> our faith, we are following in the faithful steps of those like Stephen,
> just as they were following in the trail-blazing steps of the Savior.
> May it be our joy to give ourselves for the glory of Your name."

1. Peter Riedemann, *Confession of Faith*, quoted in *Acts*, eds. Esther Chung-Kim and Todd R. Hains, vol. 6 in *Reformation Commentary on Scripture: New Testament* (IVP, 2016) [WORDsearch].
2. Adoniram Judson, "Closing Scenes in Dr. Judson's Life," in *The Missionary Magazine*, vol. XXXI, no. 2 (Boston: American Baptist Missionary Union, 1851), 38.
3. Chrysostom, *Homilies on the Acts of the Apostles* 17, quoted in *Acts*, ed. Francis Martin, with Evan Smith, vol. 5 in *Ancient Christian Commentary on Scripture: New Testament* (IVP, 2001) [WORDsearch].

"This is the boldness of speech that belongs to a man who is carrying the cross. Let us then also imitate this. For although it is not a time for war, it is always the time for boldness." [3]

JOHN CHRYSOSTOM

NOTES

SESSION 5

A SPIRIT-EMPOWERED EVANGELIST

"I want to tell people about the meaning of the cross. Not the cross that hangs on the wall or around someone's neck, but the real cross of Christ ... With all my heart I want to leave you with the truth, that he loves you, and is willing to forgive you of all your sins." [1]

BILLY GRAHAM

INDIVIDUAL STUDY

If we are to believe the secular narrative for how the world works, then most of life is a game of chance. The events that shape our lives, careers, and relationships are all an accident. We are in the right place at the right time, and suddenly we meet our spouse. A chance encounter leads to a dream job. Or worse, happenstance leads to horrible accidents, mistakes, and misery. If this story were true, then all we would have to hope for in the world is good luck, and all we could point to for what makes life good and beautiful comes by accident.

I recently heard a couple describing how they met and fell in love. It began while he was on a mission trip with his church, and she was on a mission trip with another church. They happened to be in the same place, but their trips only overlapped by a day. They met, served together for an afternoon at a medical clinic in the middle of a jungle in Central America, and went their separate ways. They thought of each other often after that trip but didn't even know the other's last name. Almost a year later, they bumped into each other at a wedding, shocked to connect again. Six months later, they were married. Ten years later, they're still going strong.

What "chance encounters" have you experienced in life or heard about?

One could fill books with stories of "chance encounters," but does it make sense that all of these stories are accidental? Is that the best description of what's going on? Does that description fit what we experience?

In the Scriptures, there are no accidents; there is no such thing as chance. Rather, chance encounters reveal themselves to be divine appointments. Throughout the Book of Acts, we see examples of "chance encounters" that prove to be providential. One example comes from Acts 8, where Philip, an evangelist and follower of Jesus, is prompted by God to go on a journey that leads to an encounter with an Ethiopian and the expansion of the kingdom. The Spirit orchestrated this meeting, and He continues this work today, leading Christians to use the Scriptures to show others Jesus so they can believe in Him for eternal life.

1 Available and Obedient

There's a thread throughout the Gospels and the Book of Acts that accentuates the reality of God's providence and planning. People find themselves suddenly prompted to hit the road, or they suddenly show up just in time to encounter Jesus or the apostles. Through these many surprise encounters, God built up His church. On one such occasion, recorded in Acts 8:26-29, a disciple of Jesus was sent to the middle of nowhere without any clue why.

> 26 An angel of the Lord spoke to Philip: "Get up and go south to the road
> that goes down from Jerusalem to Gaza." (This is the desert road.)
> 27 So he got up and went. There was an Ethiopian man, a eunuch and high
> official of Candace, queen of the Ethiopians, who was in charge of her
> entire treasury. He had come to worship in Jerusalem 28 and was sitting
> in his chariot on his way home, reading the prophet Isaiah aloud.
> 29 The Spirit told Philip, "Go and join that chariot."
> ACTS 8:26-29

When we think about sharing the gospel with a lost world, we often focus on the hostility and resistance Christians experience. That's not without justification; often the world's reaction to the gospel is visceral, violent, and harsh (as we saw in the previous session). But that's not always the case. The story of the Ethiopian reminds us that many are seeking God.

In this case, the Ethiopian knew enough to come to Jerusalem to look for God, but in many cases, people will look wherever some semblance of hope and spirituality can be found. People rush to these transcendent promises because they're hungry. They're desperate, and they will cling to whatever hope they can find. If we're attentive, we can see it happening all around us, and we just might be able to point them to something more deep, lasting, and meaningful in Jesus.

How have you witnessed people looking for God in all the wrong places?

Philip was sent by God for just such an encounter. Upon hearing the angel's command, Philip obeyed, dropping what he was doing and heading out on the road. Just a few verses earlier, Philip was enjoying a thriving ministry in Samaria. (See 8:4-8.) One could imagine that a command like this might be met with some inner resistance. Any thriving work is hard to leave, and doing so takes a great deal of faith. Philip, of course, had such faith and hit the road, traveling through the wilderness until he encountered a single chariot bearing a single Ethiopian man.

There are many reasons for this encounter not to have happened. Philip had a good thing going in Samaria; he might have just stayed home and enjoyed the community he was already a part of. The Ethiopian might not have come to Jerusalem to seek to worship God; there was surely no shortage of religious opportunity in Africa at the time.

Likewise, Philip might not have overcome the social anxiety that would likely have accompanied this encounter. Not only was the Ethiopian ethnically different from Philip, a hurdle significant enough at any point in history, but he was also of a higher social status than Philip. Luke tells us that he was a high official of "Candace, queen of the Ethiopians." Philip was an ordinary Jew living in Judea, a commoner; approaching someone of the Ethiopian's higher station wouldn't have been easy.

We could imagine a similar difficulty in approaching celebrities or high-level politicians if we saw them in public. There's a certain resistance that's natural and a fear that accompanies it. We don't want to bother "important" people, and we don't want to offend them and invoke their ire either.

The Holy Spirit sent Philip in spite of all of these things, inviting him to overcome several layers of fear and resistance. His prompting ran against common sense expectations, reminding us that the kingdom of God advances in surprising and counterintuitive ways.

What are some ways you've been surprised by how God has led you, your church, or your friends to be on mission?

How can we cultivate a heart willing to respond obediently to the Spirit's leading, no matter the risks?

2 Show Christ to Others

Philip approached the chariot and heard the Ethiopian reading the Scriptures. Listen to what he heard and how he responded.

> [30] When Philip ran up to it, he heard him reading the prophet Isaiah, and said, "Do you understand what you're reading?"
> [31] "How can I," he said, "unless someone guides me?" So he invited Philip to come up and sit with him. [32] Now the Scripture passage he was reading was this:
>
> He was led like a sheep to the slaughter,
> and as a lamb is silent before its shearer,
> so he does not open his mouth.
> [33] In his humiliation justice was denied him.
> Who will describe his generation?
> For his life is taken from the earth.
>
> [34] The eunuch said to Philip, "I ask you, who is the prophet saying this about—himself or someone else?" [35] Philip proceeded to tell him the good news about Jesus, beginning with that Scripture.
>
> ACTS 8:30-35

More evidence appears here to show how God was laying the groundwork for this encounter. The Ethiopian was immediately receptive to Philip, inviting him onto the chariot to explain the Scriptures. Not only that, he happened to be reading a passage from the Book of Isaiah that overtly talks about the sacrificial death of Jesus. The whole conversation was teed up for Philip to point this man to Jesus.

Philip didn't have the credentials of a Bible scholar or a teacher of the law; again, he was an ordinary guy. But because he was filled with the Spirit and because of what he'd seen and experienced in his own life of faith, he responded with confidence and clarity.

In the short passage that follows, we're given all we need to know about whether or not a Bible teacher is reliable. It's the simplest litmus test in the world, actually. They read a passage from Isaiah, and the Ethiopian invited Philip to explain it, asking who the passage was about. And Philip "proceeded to tell him the good news about Jesus, beginning with that Scripture."

Do you think it is possible to tell the good news about Jesus from anywhere in the Scriptures? Why or why not?

Bible teachers who are faithful to both their task and their text will always end up talking about Jesus. The whole story of the Bible, from one end to the other, points to Him. The story of Israel and the whole of the Old Testament are about anticipating Jesus. We see it in how they longed for a king, though all their kings fell short of the glory they aspired to. We see it in the high demands of the law, which no man can attain. We see it in the countless laments in the Psalms and Prophets, where the brokenness of the world is displayed and the people cry out, "How long, Lord?"

Jesus manages to embody all that the Old Testament longs for and points to. Even the broader story of the Old Testament—exile from the garden of Eden, longing for the promised land, exile (again) at the hands of the Babylonians—points to Jesus as the conquering King who defeats Satan, sin, and death, and brings us back home to God.

We can judge the faithfulness of Bible teaching, including our own, by this simple question: Who is the hero of the story? If it's anyone or anything but Jesus, we've missed the point. Too often our conversations around the Bible get tangled up in the ethics of the Bible or the facts of the Bible. We're eager to be "right" about this point or that one, and we lose sight of the real point and purpose of the Bible.

Philip's faith was his most important credential as a Bible teacher. His faith was what made him able and willing to follow the lead of the Spirit as he was sent here and there, and it was what made him able to hear God's Word and see Jesus in it.

What are some reasons we might feel intimidated to try and explain the Scriptures to an unbeliever?

How can we grow in our ability and confidence to share Christ from the Scriptures?

3 Lead Others to Respond

The Ethiopian official was clearly moved by the story that Philip shared and was eager to respond, as Acts 8:36-40 tells us.

> 36 As they were traveling down the road, they came to some water. The eunuch said, "Look, there's water. What would keep me from being baptized?" 38 So he ordered the chariot to stop, and both Philip and the eunuch went down into the water, and he baptized him. 39 When they came up out of the water, the Spirit of the Lord carried Philip away, and the eunuch did not see him any longer but went on his way rejoicing. 40 Philip appeared in Azotus, and he was traveling and preaching the gospel in all the towns until he came to Caesarea.
>
> ACTS 8:36-40

All of the elements of true conversion are on display here. The Ethiopian was eager to believe, not compelled, and certainly not pressured to convert. Philip had explained how the passage of Scripture he was reading pointed to Jesus, whose death and resurrection reconciles us to God. It seems he also explained enough so that the Ethiopian was eager to identify with Jesus through baptism.

"What would keep me from being baptized?" he asked. That question was crucial. Some might have offered a variety of reasons not to baptize him: he was an Ethiopian, not an ethnic Jew; he was a eunuch; he was a foreigner. But of course, Philip, filled with the Spirit, didn't put any stock in those hindrances. It is clear the Ethiopian believed what he heard about Jesus—that He is the Lamb of God who takes away the sin of the world—and so, Philip baptized him without delay.

Evangelism and conversion really are that simple. We can share "just the facts," however, without asking people to make something of them. But the goal of evangelism isn't just to share what we know with people; it's to invite them to join us in following Jesus. The hope of an evangelist is to help someone see Jesus as Lord and see that His life, death, and resurrection takes away the sins of the world and brings us home to God the Father. In Philip's short conversation with the Ethiopian, this miracle happened. He saw Jesus as Lord and was ready to follow Him into the waters of baptism.

How do the details of this story fulfill Jesus' Great Commission to His disciples? (See Matt. 28:18-20.)

As this story concludes, we see the two parted ways even more suddenly than they came together. What's implied here is that something more than meets the eye took Philip away. It's as if the Spirit carried him away and deposited him in Azotus. The Ethiopian, filled with the joy of being a new Christian and filled with the Holy Spirit, went on his own way back to his home, where one must imagine that the Spirit continued His work and the story of Jesus spread and grew roots in Africa.

The next leg in Philip's journey, though, continued his ministry of expanding the kingdom among the Gentiles. Azotus, where he suddenly appeared, was thirty miles away and wasn't a Jewish enclave. The kingdom's expansion to the non-Jewish world had officially begun. This expansion of the kingdom happened because of a willing and submissive heart that obeyed God's call to leave the thriving ministry in Samaria and seek out one person who needed to hear the gospel. And this encounter no doubt fueled the joyful overflow of gospel proclamation from town to town as Philip traveled from Azotus to Caesarea.

Why is calling for a response vital when sharing the gospel of Jesus Christ with others?

What are some ways you can do the work of a Spirit-empowered evangelist in the coming days?

GROUP STUDY

Warm Up

When have you experienced a moment you didn't want to end?

We all experience a hunger to make the good times last. As Christians, we feel it sometimes at the end of a retreat or in the midst of a rich worship experience, or we find ourselves looking back with a nostalgic fondness on moments like these in our past. Sometimes we refer to them as "mountaintop experiences."

It is always tempting to cling to spiritually-rich, joy-filled moments. In Matthew 17, when Jesus allowed Peter, James, and John to witness His transfiguration and the appearance of Moses and Elijah, we see that temptation at work. Peter offered to build shelters for them, as if to say, "Let's just stay here and keep this thing going." Almost as soon as he said it, though, the moment ended—Jesus' physical appearance returned to normal and Moses and Elijah were gone.

The Bible shows us that these moments, as rich as they are, are temporary. We are not meant to "stay put" in the past or even the present but to keep moving forward. For Philip, ministry in Samaria was thriving, but the Lord called him away to meet the Ethiopian.

In what ways can you use those rich, joy-filled moments from your past to inspire you as you keep moving forward?

"It is true that God may have called you to be exactly where you are. But it's absolutely vital to grasp that He didn't call you there so you could settle in and live out your life in comfort and superficial peace. His purposes are not random or arbitrary. If you are still alive on this planet, it's because He has something for you to do."[2]

FRANCIS CHAN

Discussion

1. How have you witnessed people looking for God in all the wrong places?

2. What are some ways you've been surprised by how God has led you, your church, or your friends to be on mission?

3. How can we cultivate a heart willing to respond obediently to the Spirit's leading, no matter the risks?

4. Do you think it is possible to tell the good news about Jesus from anywhere in the Scriptures? Why or why not?

5. What are some reasons we might feel intimidated to try and explain the Scriptures to an unbeliever?

6. How can we grow in our ability and confidence to share Christ from the Scriptures?

7. Why is calling for a response vital when sharing the gospel of Jesus Christ with others?

8. What are some ways you can do the work of a Spirit-empowered evangelist in the coming days?

Conclusion

The Spirit, like the wind, is always on the move, quietly leading the church and its members to take each proceeding step and advance the work of the kingdom. Life in the Spirit is never about arriving but about continuing with a hopeful eye toward the day when the gospel has been carried to every corner of the world and the whole earth is filled with the glory of God.

A "chance encounter," as the world often sees it, might be a crucial moment in someone's life. There are no coincidences. But before we let this make us anxious or fearful of missing a key moment, let's not forget that we never experience these moments alone. The Holy Spirit accompanies us, guides us, and provides us with these opportunities. He empowers us for this work with boldness and with words, and He has already gone ahead of us to soften hearts and open ears to hear the good news of Jesus Christ. So as we go our ways in the world, let us go and make disciples for Jesus.

Spend some time praying this for you and for your group:

"God, help us remember that the most ordinary of circumstances might be a divine appointment. Thank You for the promise that we never enter these situations on our own. You send Your Spirit to fill us with all we need. May we go forth, bold and empowered, to share the good news with those whose eyes and ears You have prepared in advance."

1. Billy Graham, quoted in "40 Courageous Quotes from Billy Graham," by Debbie McDaniel, crosswalk.com/faith/spiritual-life/inspiring-quotes/40-courageous-quotes-from-billy-graham.html.
2. Francis Chan with Danae Yankoski, *Forgotten God* (Colorado Springs: David C. Cook, 2009), 92.
3. R. Kent Hughes, *Acts: The Church Afire, in Preaching the Word* (Wheaton: Crossway, 2008) [WORDsearch].

"From ground level we see the role of human obedience. Would the eunuch have been saved even if Philip had disobeyed? The question is irrelevant. God chooses to use human obedience to carry out his plan. Exactly whom he uses or how is incidental … there are all kinds of 'chance' meetings ready to take place in a life that is sensitive and obedient to God's leading."[3]

R. KENT HUGHES

NOTES

SESSION 6

A SPIRIT-EMPOWERED MESSAGE

"Never ... lose heart in the power of the gospel. Do not believe that there exists any man, much less any race of men, for whom the gospel is not fitted."[1]

CHARLES SPURGEON

INDIVIDUAL STUDY

Many years ago, I was a volunteer leader at a youth ministry at a dignified, quiet, suburban church. One Wednesday night at our youth group gathering, a handful of new kids showed up. They'd been invited by the youth minister, promising the typical youth group fare: pizza, games, music, and a time for talking about Jesus. These kids didn't fit the mold of most of the church's well-heeled members.

At first, the church welcomed them, and eventually, many of them came to faith and got baptized. They invited more of their friends. The youth group started to look different, and the youth group kids were excited, learning what it meant to live on mission. Something was stirring in the community, and it was beautiful.

But some in the church were troubled by these developments. Tension began to build and conversations took place until the day the church fired the youth minister. The Wednesday night youth group meeting was disbanded. Kids that still showed up on Sundays were scolded if they weren't dressed appropriately, and of course, those kids left. Soon things returned to the comfortable familiarity that the church had known before.

> **What boundaries have you seen or experienced that separated Christians from one another? That wrongly kept the unchurched from hearing the gospel?**

The gospel resists and tears down the boundaries that often separate people in the world, and the writers of the New Testament were often at pains to confront the church when it failed to unite around the gospel and break these walls down. Peter, who struggled with such issues himself, learned the importance of calling the church to brotherly unity, but his journey toward unity took the Holy Spirit paving the way in the heart of a Gentile and then in his own heart. With God, there is no favoritism, and salvation is offered to people from every tribe, tongue, and nation.

1 God Cultivates a Heart

The Holy Spirit began the work of taking the gospel to the Gentiles and helping the fledgling church see this as God's plan. In Acts 10:1-8, we see that He began a new stage of this work with a man named Cornelius.

> [1] There was a man in Caesarea named Cornelius, a centurion of what was called the Italian Regiment. [2] He was a devout man and feared God along with his whole household. He did many charitable deeds for the Jewish people and always prayed to God. [3] About three in the afternoon he distinctly saw in a vision an angel of God who came in and said to him, "Cornelius."
>
> [4] Staring at him in awe, he said, "What is it, Lord?"
>
> The angel told him, "Your prayers and your acts of charity have ascended as a memorial offering before God. [5] Now send men to Joppa and call for Simon, who is also named Peter. [6] He is lodging with Simon, a tanner, whose house is by the sea."
> [7] When the angel who spoke to him had gone, he called two of his household servants and a devout soldier, who was one of those who attended him. [8] After explaining everything to them, he sent them to Joppa.
> ACTS 10:1-8

Cornelius seems to be someone who revered God for a long time. He was a Roman living in Judea and overseeing several hundred Roman soldiers stationed at Caesarea. He was not a foot soldier but more like a battalion commander, a person with political and military power at his disposal.

God had been cultivating a spiritual hunger in Cornelius, and when He sent an angel to speak with Cornelius, He commended his good heart and good work—describing his efforts as a "memorial offering," a worthy sacrifice before the Lord. In the Roman Empire, where religions abounded, religious performance abounded too. It was a pluralistic and inclusive culture around religion, which invited Romans to participate in the worship of whatever gods happened to be important to them. For Cornelius, though, something more was at work. He wasn't simply doing his religious duty and going through the motions. Instead, his heart was moved to worship God. As the psalmist pointed out, mere material sacrifice doesn't impress God, but a broken and contrite heart does. (See Ps. 51:17.)

God commended Cornelius for this greater sacrifice of the heart and invited him to know Him further.

Notice how God drew Cornelius to a deeper relationship with Himself. He didn't simply reveal Jesus to Cornelius in his vision. Instead, He commanded Cornelius to meet with Peter, one of Jesus' disciples. God-fearing Cornelius obeyed, gathering some servants and sending them off to find Peter in Joppa, where the angel said Peter would be.

> **Why do you think God chooses to use Christians to spread the gospel?**

If we pay attention to what motivates and attracts people to their various religious practices, we might discover hearts that, like Cornelius, are truly seeking the face of God. We might discover hearts that long for truth. We might discover people with an awareness of their spiritual poverty, people who are looking under every leaf for the possibility of an encounter with the Divine. At the same time, we shouldn't expect people to find what they're looking for apart from God's own miraculous intervention. Moreover, we shouldn't expect them to find God apart from His church.

That's one of the most surprising things about Cornelius' story. As pious as he was and as much as his heart seemed to be in the right place, Cornelius needed more than good motives to find God. He needed the church, the community of faithful saints who are filled with the Spirit and telling the world about Jesus.

> **What are some ways you see non-Christians seeking God in the world around you?**

> **How might you point them to Jesus in light of their misguided efforts to find God?**

2 A New Reality

Meanwhile, the apostle Peter had a vision of his own that would challenge his understanding of God and His image-bearers.

> ⁹ The next day, as they were traveling and nearing the city, Peter went up to pray on the roof about noon. ¹⁰ He became hungry and wanted to eat, but while they were preparing something, he fell into a trance. ¹¹ He saw heaven opened and an object that resembled a large sheet coming down, being lowered by its four corners to the earth. ¹² In it were all the four-footed animals and reptiles of the earth, and the birds of the sky. ¹³ A voice said to him, "Get up, Peter; kill and eat."
>
> ¹⁴ "No, Lord!" Peter said. "For I have never eaten anything impure and ritually unclean."
>
> ¹⁵ Again, a second time, the voice said to him, "What God has made clean, do not call impure." ¹⁶ This happened three times, and suddenly the object was taken up into heaven.
>
> ACTS 10:9-16

This was not your average "hungry guy dreams of food" dream, and many aspects of this event mark it as significant. For starters, it was not a dream at all; it was a vision, something the Lord gave Peter as he was up on the roof praying. He didn't fall asleep, and he didn't stumble upon God's revelation. Peter heard from God because he was seeking God. In and of itself, this is an important point. Like Cornelius, Peter was ready to hear from God precisely because he was seeking God. It's an encouraging message for both believer and unbeliever alike—seek the face of God!

In the vision God gave him, Peter saw something coming down from the heavens, lowered by "four corners." More than describing the geometrical shape of this sheet, this phrase indicates that something with big implications was happening. The sheet with four corners recalls the four corners of the earth (see Isa. 11:12; Rev. 7:1); whatever God was revealing to Peter had world-spanning consequences.

In the sheet with four corners being lowered from heaven, Peter saw all the animals and birds of the earth represented. Peter, who lived according to the rules and traditions of Jewish culture, would have been scandalized by this sight and even more scandalized by the command to "kill and eat." Dietary laws were integral to Jewish national and cultural identity. God gave the law to Israel as a way of distinguishing them from the pagan culture of their neighbors, and breaking with this pattern was seen as dishonoring to God, family, and nation.

So Peter's response to the voice of the Lord was a firm no. Perhaps Peter thought he was being tested—was his hunger so strong that it could overcome his convictions about the dietary laws he had kept from birth? The voice responded by telling him that God had made these animals clean and Peter must not call them impure anymore.

> What are some ways God has surprised you or disrupted your expectations?

Peter's vision marked a turning point in the life of the church. Luke tells the story in a way that shows us God's providence at work. Cornelius' heart was being drawn to God just as Peter's heart was being opened to new possibilities. Something was about to change; some expectation, some sense of Jewish identity, was about to shift.

The command to ignore Israel's dietary laws and "kill and eat" indicated that the time of Israel's being separate from the rest of the world on account of the Law of Moses had come to an end. What would set them apart from the world now was their faith in Jesus, not their cultural and religious traditions. Peter would soon discover that in this new reality, he had more in common with a Gentile centurion who trusted in Jesus than with a Jewish brother or sister who didn't believe.

> How should we reconcile the details of this story with the truth that God never changes?

> What traditions might we need to reject or hold loosely so we don't call impure what God has made clean?

3 Welcome All Who Believe

As Peter was contemplating his vision and its meaning, the three men Cornelius sent arrived at Simon the tanner's house. They invited Peter to come to Caesarea to meet Cornelius, recounting his visit from an angel, and the next day they set out. It's telling that Peter went along with them. As he later explained to Cornelius, "You know it's forbidden for a Jewish man to associate with or visit a foreigner" (Acts 10:28). Peter only went because he understood his vision—God was telling him that Gentiles are no longer unclean and should not be excluded from the good news of the gospel.

34 Peter began to speak: "Now I truly understand that God doesn't show favoritism, 35 but in every nation the person who fears him and does what is right is acceptable to him. 36 He sent the message to the Israelites, proclaiming the good news of peace through Jesus Christ—he is Lord of all. 37 You know the events that took place throughout all Judea, beginning from Galilee after the baptism that John preached: 38 how God anointed Jesus of Nazareth with the Holy Spirit and with power, and how he went about doing good and healing all who were under the tyranny of the devil, because God was with him. 39 We ourselves are witnesses of everything he did in both the Judean country and in Jerusalem, and yet they killed him by hanging him on a tree. 40 God raised up this man on the third day and caused him to be seen, 41 not by all the people, but by us whom God appointed as witnesses, who ate and drank with him after he rose from the dead. 42 He commanded us to preach to the people and to testify that he is the one appointed by God to be the judge of the living and the dead. 43 All the prophets testify about him that through his name everyone who believes in him receives forgiveness of sins."

44 While Peter was still speaking these words, the Holy Spirit came down on all those who heard the message. 45 The circumcised believers who had come with Peter were amazed because the gift of the Holy Spirit had been poured out even on the Gentiles. 46 For they heard them speaking in other tongues and declaring the greatness of God. Then Peter responded, 47 "Can anyone withhold water and prevent these people from being baptized, who have received the Holy Spirit just as we have?" 48 He commanded them to be baptized in the name of Jesus Christ. Then they asked him to stay for a few days.

ACTS 10:34-48

Peter preached the gospel, covering the entire story of Jesus' life and ministry, His death, and His resurrection, and while he was still speaking about these things, the Holy Spirit descended upon all those who heard the gospel message. Cornelius' whole household no longer just feared God but believed in Jesus, and as the Spirit was poured out on them, they erupted in ecstatic expressions of His presence and gifts. As with Philip and the Ethiopian in the previous session, Peter couldn't think of any reason to withhold baptism from this Spirit-filled community comprised of Gentiles.

How have you been surprised by God's grace getting through to someone and calling that person to faith in Jesus?

We should consider how this story might be re-framed in our own contexts. For any number of cultural, political, racial, and social reasons, Christians throughout the history of the church have had to wrestle with the temptation to write off certain people as improbable Christians, if not impossible. We assume "that person" would never get saved or "that group" is too hostile to the gospel. We assume those who are different from us would be unwilling to hear us. We assume that those who differ from us on politics are too ideologically different to receive the good news. And sometimes we just assume that certain people are too evil, too stupid, or too prideful to accept Christ.

It is always a mistake to think this way. God has long been in the business of surprising His people. Seeing that pattern so clearly in Scripture—from David becoming king, to Jesus being the Messiah, to a gruff fisherman being the catalyst for the conversion of a Roman centurion and his entire household—we ought to be eager to see that pattern in our ordinary lives. The gospel once surprised us with grace. Through us, we might just get to see it surprise us (and the world around us) again and again.

What groups of people might we be prone to write off as too resistant to the gospel?

What are some specific ways this story should change our perspective?

GROUP STUDY

Warm Up

In our day, we could find many people who are seeking after God but don't know Jesus. We live in an age where, alongside rigid secularism, religion abounds. There's a kind of feel-good "God is love" religion whose concepts of God are vague and simplistic. There's a kind of power-of-positive-thinking religion that shows up in many different forms. As Christians, we can certainly find elements of these religions that are objectionable, but we should be careful not to dismiss the people who practice them too quickly and not to be too simplistic in our thoughts about them.

We should pay attention to the ways their hearts are seeking God, and when we see good things at work in their hearts, such as humility, brokenness, love, and charity, we can applaud them. But we can't stop there; we must also invite them to think about Jesus, and we can invite them to come to know Him in the community of His church.

The next time you encounter someone like this—or maybe you already know someone—how might you take their misguided efforts to find God and point him or her to Jesus instead?

"The Gospel is open to all; the most respectable sinner has no more claim on it than the worst."[2]

DAVID MARTYN LLOYD-JONES

Discussion

1. Why do you think God chooses to use Christians to spread the gospel?

2. What are some ways you see non-Christians seeking God in the world around you?

3. How might you point them to Jesus in light of their misguided efforts to find God?

4. What are some ways God has surprised you or disrupted your expectations?

5. How should we reconcile the details of this story with the truth that God never changes?

6. How have you been surprised by God's grace getting through to someone and calling that person to faith in Jesus?

7. What groups of people might we be prone to write off as too resistant to the gospel?

8. What are some specific ways this story should change our perspective?

Conclusion

While the story of Peter and Cornelius might be familiar, we may still be unaware of the way implicit biases have taken up residence in our own hearts. So like the early church, we're wise to pause, examine our consciences, and ask whether our attitude toward people—especially those who are not like us for racial, social, economic, or political reasons—might be hindering the unity of the body of Christ. It's a tough question but one worth pressing into for the sake of a church that knows no favoritism or distinctions for those in Jesus.

Spend some time praying this for you and for your group:

> "God, help us to be a reflection of You. May we never show favoritism but instead proclaim the message of Jesus' death and resurrection to all people, to celebrate what You have done in our lives, and to welcome believers into Your family, regardless of their ethnicity."

1. C. H. Spurgeon, "The Cripple at Lystra," in *Spurgeon's Sermons*, 8th series (New York: Sheldon and Company, 1865), 244.
2. David Martyn Lloyd-Jones, quoted in *The Westminster Collection of Christian Quotations*, comp. and ed. Martin H. Manser (Louisville: Westminster John Knox, 2001), 150.
3. J. D. Greear, *Gospel: Recovering the Power That Made Christianity Revolutionary* (Nashville: B&H, 2011), 55.

"My identity and my security are not in my spiritual progress. My identity and my security are in God's acceptance of me given as a gift in Christ." [3]

J. D. GREEAR

NOTES

SMALL-GROUP TIPS

Reading through this section and utilizing the suggested principles and practices will greatly enhance the group experience. First is to accept your limitations. You cannot transform a life. Your group must be devoted to the Bible, the Holy Spirit, and the power of Christian community. In doing so your group will have all the tools necessary to draw closer to God and to each other—and to experience heart transformation.

GENERAL TIPS:

- Prepare for each meeting by reviewing the material, praying for each group member, and asking the Holy Spirit to work through you as you point to Jesus each week.

- Make new attendees feel welcome.

- Think of ways to connect with group members away from group time. The amount of participation you have during your group meetings is directly related to the time you take to connect with your group members away from the group meeting. Consider sending emails, texts, or social networking messages encouraging members in their personal devotion times prior to the session.

MATERIALS NEEDED:

- Bible

- Bible study book

- Pen/pencil

PROVIDE RESOURCES FOR GUESTS:

- An inexpensive way to make first-time guests feel welcome is to provide them a copy of your Bible study book. Estimate how many first-time guests you can expect during the course of your study, and secure that number of books. What about people who have not yet visited your group? You can encourage them to visit by providing a copy of the Bible study book.